AF268684

Written By: Patricia F. Braga
Illustrated By: Patricia F. Braga

ISBN 978-1-7782006-2-5(ebook)
ISBN 978-1-7782006-3-2 (paperback)
ISBN 978-1-7782006-1-8(hardback)

http://author.patriciabraga.com

Tales of the Forest

vol. 1

written and illustrated by

Patricia F. Braga

This book I dedicate to my children Oliver and Noah, who always get the best in me and inspire me everyday to be creative to draw and write stories.

The Fox and the Toucan

Once upon a time, the fox invited the toucan for dinner at her place. Although they were friends, the fox was well known for her cleverness and for taking advantage of everything. So she prepared a porridge and served it over a flat rock for them to eat. She knew it would be hard for the toucan to pick up the food with his long beak.

"There would be more food left for me", the fox thought. The poor toucan tried very hard to eat his meal, pecking and pecking, but he couldn't pick up the food with his long beak. He ended up hurting himself. Very angry, the toucan decided to give the fox a taste of its own medicine.

"My friend, since you invited me to join you for dinner the other day, it's my turn to reciprocate. Come to my house today at dinnertime. I'll offer you a nice warm meal," said the toucan. All excited, the fox couldn't refuse the invitation.

The toucan then prepared a soup and served it in a long and narrow jar. As soon as the starving fox arrived, She tried and tried to reach the soup inside the long jar, licking only a little bit that had fallen on the table. Meanwhile, the toucan was enjoying the food.

He looked at the frustrated fox and said, "My dear friend, now you know how I felt, because you did the same to me." The toucan grabbed a plate and poured some of the soup to serve it to the starving fox. The fox apologized for her behavior. She then understood that you have to put yourself in someone else's shoes to understand how they feel.

The
Alligator
and the
Bird

In the middle of the forest, there's a swamp where a giant alligator used to live. His big scale-covered body and his big mouth full of sharp teeth made him the most feared creature in the area. Every living animal in that part of the forest was afraid of him.

The alligator was very proud of how strong he was. Nothing scared him! No animal in the forest would dare to defy him with those scary teeth. He was very confident about how superior he was compared to the other creatures.

One day, while taking a nap after his lunch, the alligator jumped as if lightning had struck him on the head. "Oooooouch!" screamed the alligator, putting his hand over his big jaw. There was some food stuck between his sharp teeth, which was causing pain. The alligator's screamed so loud that it could be heard everywhere.

All the little animals ran to hide in the bushes, thinking that the giant animal was attacking them. "Somebody, help me!" the alligator continued to scream. No one came to help him, because every living creature around was too scared to get closer. No matter how strong and big he was, the alligator couldn't do anything to help himself. He needed someone else's help.

Realizing he was all alone, the alligator sat and started to cry. One little bird, feeling sad for the suffering alligator, decided to approach him very carefully. "Mr. Alligator, do you want me to help you?" whispered the bird. The alligator immediately stopped crying and nodded his head in agreement while staring at the tiny creature in front of him.

He showed his hurting teeth to the bird. "Please keep your mouth wide open while I remove what is causing you pain." the bird said fearfully. The brave bird got into that giant mouth and started to remove the food stuck in the alligator's teeth. As soon as the bird had removed the last piece of food, the alligator breathed in relief.

"Thank you, my little friend. I thought I would never need somebody's help, but here you are to prove me wrong." the alligator said. After that day, the alligator understood that no one is so strong that they would never need somebody else's help. He also understood the importance of cooperation between living creatures.

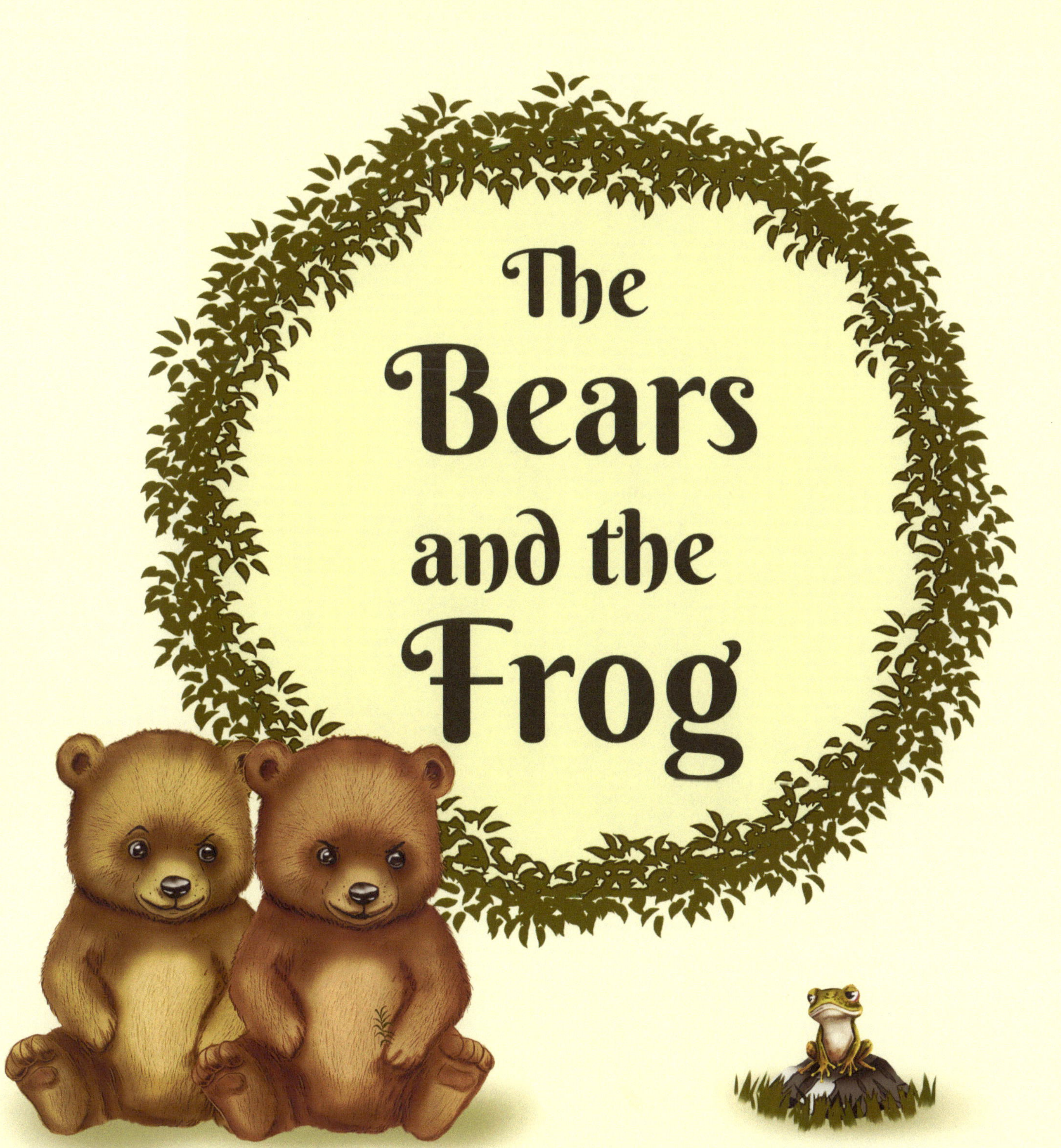

The Bears and the Frog

On a sunny day, two naughty bears were resting under the shadow of a tree when they saw a sleeping frog nearby. They decided to have some fun and started to tease him. The bears grabbed the frog and began to insult and threaten him.

"Let's throw him to the alligators!" one of the bears said. Despite the scary situation, the frog appeared to remain calm. He smiled at them and started to whistle a song. The bears couldn't understand why he was so calm, and they intensified their threats.

"Let's eat him alive!" one of the bears threatened. "Let's throw him in the fire!" the other bear screamed. The frog continued to ignore them. Nothing could take away the frog's peace. At one moment, one of the bears raged, "Let's drown him in the water then!" The bear was out of patience with the frog's calm look.

After hearing that, the frog screamed in despair, "Ooooh no! Please don't do it! I'll do anything, but please don't do it! I don't know how to swim." The bears, seeing that the frog had finally gotten scared about something, said, "Ah, so that's it! Let's throw him into the water!"

They pulled the frog's legs so they could throw him into the water. What they didn't know was that the frog was indeed a very good swimmer. When they threw him into the water, the frog started to laugh at them.

He swam very fast, far away from there. The frog was very smart. He didn't let his fear take control of the situation and remained calm. The tranquility of the frog allowed him to escape the bad situation.

The Rabbit and the Reflex

In the middle of the woods, there was a family of rabbits living in the hollow of a tree. Mommy Rabbit asked the little rabbit to get some carrots for dinner. "Get only what you can carry and come back home," advised Mommy Rabbit. The little rabbit was all excited to be responsible for bringing dinner to his family, so he left to search for the carrots. He took with him a basket so he could put all the carrots in it.

His basket was full of carrots when he decided to go home. On his way back, he came across a small lake. The shiny water was so enchanting that the rabbit went closer to see it. As soon as the rabbit took a look at the water, he saw his image holding the carrots.

Thinking that it was another rabbit with lots of carrots, he tried to take the carrots from the rabbit he saw reflected in the water. Because of that, he lost his balance, dropping his basket full of carrots in the water.

The little rabbit sat very sadly on a tree trunk. He wouldn't be able to bring food to his family that day. He remembered his mom's advice about only carrying what he could take, and he understood that because of his greedy desire to get more carrots, he had ended up with none.

The
Worst
Friend

One day, two squirrels were traveling through the forest.
They had been gone a few days, and they were very tired.
The squirrels were sitting on a rock when one of them saw a big
bear approaching. Immediately, the first squirrel quickly climbed
a tree and hid, while the other squirrel was left alone.

As the bear came closer, the second squirrel threw himself on the ground, pretending to be dead. The squirrel knew that some predators do not attack dead prey. Trembling, fearing for his life, the second squirrel kept quiet while the bear got closer and closer to him.

The hidden squirrel saw his friend was in danger. Yet, he wanted to avoid drawing the bear's attention to himself. The bear approached the squirrel on the ground and started to smell him, getting even closer to his face. When the squirrel thought it would be the end of him, the bear whispered something in his ear and left.

As soon as the bear was far enough away, the first squirrel came down from the tree. "What did he tell you?" he asked. "The bear gave me some advice. He told me not to hang out with people who abandon their friends in times of trouble," answered the second squirrel, while looking in disappointment at his so called friend.

The End

About the Author

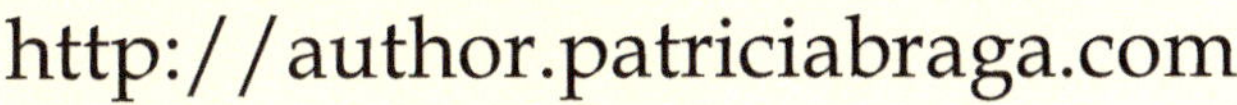

Patricia Braga is a talented illustrator and software engineer born in Brazil and currently living in Canada. With a passion for creativity and a knack for storytelling, she recently ventured into the world of writing where she brings a unique perspective to her work. She initiated her path into children's books literature motivated by her childhood passion for children's books. Being a mom of two boys and having illustrated more than fifteen children's books, she always had this public as a guide when creating something, wheather is an illustration or a story. Patricia's joyful spirit shines through in her writing and in her illustrations, captivating readers with her imaginative plots and vibrant characters. Get ready to be swept away on a literary adventure with Patricia Braga as your guide!

www.ingramcontent.com/pod-product-compliance
Lightning Source LLC
Chambersburg PA
CBHW042125030726

47599CB00002B/349